FREEDOM'S SONS

The True Story of the
AMISTAD Mutiny

FREEDOM'S SONS

The True Story of the *AMISTAD* Mutiny

SUZANNE JURMAIN

LOTHROP, LEE & SHEPARD BOOKS ✳ MORROW

NEW YORK

Published by Lothrop, Lee & Shepard Books
an imprint of Morrow Junior Books
a division of William Morrow and Company, Inc.
1350 Avenue of the Americas, New York, NY 10019
www.williammorrow.com

Printed in the United States of America.

10 9 8 7 6 5 4 3

Library of Congress Cataloging-in-Publication Data
Jurmain, Suzanne.
Freedom's sons: the true story of the Amistad mutiny/Suzanne Jurmain.
p. cm.
Includes bibliographical references and index.
ISBN 0-688-11072-X
1. Slavery—United States—Insurrections, etc.   2. Amistad (Schooner).
3. Antislavery movements—United States.   I. Title.
E447.J87 1998   326'.0973—dc21
97-37258   CIP AC

FOR SARA AND DAVID:
another story.

Contents

Eight pages of photographs follow page 64.

FREEDOM'S SONS

The True Story of the
AMISTAD Mutiny

CHAPTER 1

⟨⟩◆⟨⟩

MENDE LAND,
WEST AFRICA

On a winter day, probably sometime in January 1839, a gang of four trappers made their way across the West African countryside. They were local men, armed with guns and knives. At the moment, they were within striking distance of their target: a rice farmer who was working on a nearby road. He was a tall, powerful man about twenty-five years of age—but it was four against one.

The trappers grabbed him. They tied his right hand to his neck, clamped a collar around his throat, and leashed him—like a dog—to a string of other captives.

Cinque,* a freeborn man from a tiny village in the Mende region of West Africa, had just become a slave.

---

*The African version of this name is Sengbe Pieh. The most common American version, Cinque, is pronounced SIN-kay.

CHAPTER 2

———◆———

THE ROAD
TO THE COAST

Slavery was an ancient practice that existed in many parts of the world at some time during history. In Mende Land and other parts of nineteenth-century Africa, criminals and prisoners of war were often forced to work as slaves. Even ordinary citizens could be seized and sold if they failed to pay their bills, and Cinque later admitted that he'd been captured because he hadn't paid a debt.

Publicly, he never said much more about the attack or about what happened in the days that followed. When asked, Cinque just explained that his first owner, a man named Mayagilalo, kept him three days and then sent him on to a new master who lived about a hundred miles away.

He didn't describe that journey or talk about how it felt to lose his freedom and leave his family and his home. Cinque said only that he was taken to the seacoast kingdom of the Vai and handed over to his second owner: a Vai prince named Manna Siaka. Then, for the next few weeks, he waited to see what Siaka was going to do with him.

Almost anything was possible. In Africa, some slaves were scorned and abused; others, however, enjoyed many of the same rights and privileges as free citizens. They could own property, testify in court, inherit wealth, or even marry a member of the master's family. Although most had to work in mines and fields, some slaves became warriors. A few became important government officials, and in Nigeria an Igbo slave named Ja Ja became a king. Treatment varied from master to master and from nation to nation. The Mandingo were said to be "remarkably kind" to slaves. The Chewa humiliated them. The Vai often sold them to foreign traders.

The African slave trade was a big business—and a very old one. For more than a thousand years—between about 800 and 1890—Arab traders shipped a stream of captives from the northern and eastern parts of Africa to markets in the Middle East and Asia. European sailors took their first cargo of twelve West African slaves to Lisbon in 1441.

Half a century later, after Christopher Columbus reached the New World, Spanish colonists found that they needed an army of workers to dig mines and plant crops in the Americas. They tried to enslave the local inhabitants, but their Native American laborers died by the thousands of disease, overwork, and cruelty. To take their place, the Spanish began to import African slaves. Other European settlers quickly followed their example, and the demand for slaves skyrocketed. Between the 1500s and the 1880s, some twelve and a half million men, women, and children—mostly from West Africa—were shipped across the Atlantic to the New World.

Because few ship captains were willing to stay ashore long enough to capture slaves, most bought their human cargoes from European traders, local merchants, or rulers who lived near the coast. Kings rarely wanted to sell their own subjects, but some were willing to turn over their slaves or prisoners of war to foreign traders. Wars were sometimes fought in part to acquire captives, and armed gangs of slavers attacked towns, ambushed travelers, and kidnapped children on village streets. Some African rulers refused to take part in the traffic. Some, like King Afonso of Kongo, bravely tried to stop it. But others—like the Vai kings—used slave trade profits to fight wars and conquer new territory.

Manna Siaka and his father were in the business of selling captives, and after about a month they sold Cinque. They sent him up the coast to a trading station called Lomboko. There, Siaka's men turned him over to Pedro Blanco, a Spaniard who made millions by supplying sea captains with ready-to-travel cargoes of slaves.

CHAPTER 3

ACROSS
THE ATLANTIC

At Lomboko, hundreds of slaves were chained in gloomy roofed pens built of thick logs bolted together by rows of iron bars. Armed guards patrolled the entire station: a large complex of offices, jails, and watchtowers hidden in the thickets of a dismal mangrove swamp at the mouth of the Gallinas River.

During the two months he spent in the Lomboko pens, Cinque gradually got to know some of his fellow captives. He met Grabeau, a short, sharp-witted trader who spoke four African languages; Burna, who knew a few words of English; and dozens of other men who had once been farmers, traders, craftsmen, or even wealthy gentlemen. Some, like Cinque, had been enslaved for minor crimes or debt. Others were prisoners of war, and many had been kidnapped by bands of slavers. They came from different nations and spoke a variety of languages. Most were in their teens or early twenties. Some had never seen white men before.

In March or early April 1839, Blanco sold Cinque, Grabeau, Burna, and a group of other Africans to the captain of a Portuguese slave ship called the *Teçora*.

The procedure for loading human cargo was fairly standard. Guards fed the prisoners and shaved their heads. Then they drove the slaves onto a beach where dugout canoes waited to ferry the captives out to a sailing ship anchored close to shore.

But the operation didn't always go smoothly. Men and women from inland areas sometimes panicked at their first sight of the dark, heaving ocean. Some slaves, guessing that they were about to leave home forever, struggled or tried to hang back. Some even tried to strangle themselves with their own chains or jump into the shark-infested waters. But the slavers forced their captives into the canoes and watched the paddlers ferry them out to the ship.

On board, the ship's captain and his crew waited

for the first arrivals. For the sailors, getting ready for sea was a tricky business. Prisoners sometimes mutinied when they were brought aboard. Stowing adequate supplies of food and water was difficult. And there was one other problem: By 1839, shipping African slaves to the New World was a criminal offense.

Great Britain, the United States, and most major European nations had recently outlawed the African slave trade. Britain enforced the ban, and British Navy patrols often seized slave ships as they left the African coast. Britain, however, didn't have enough manpower to stop every slaver. Ships like the *Teçora* ran the blockade regularly. But every extra minute spent near African shores increased the risk of being caught, and it was important to get the cargo aboard quickly.

When the canoes pulled alongside, sailors usually hauled the prisoners on deck, stripped them naked, and clamped heavy iron fetters on their arms and legs. Aboard the *Teçora*, Cinque, Grabeau, Burna, and about seven hundred others were chained in pairs and jammed into the ship's tiny hold. There was barely room enough for them to sit. It was almost impossible to lie down. A man could stand only if he bent double.

After the cargo loading was complete, the captain ordered his crew to hoist sail, and the *Teçora* set out for the Spanish colony of Cuba, over four thousand nautical miles away. Depending on weather, the journey would take anywhere from three weeks to three months.

Down in the dark overcrowded holds of slave ships, those who couldn't reach the latrine buckets sometimes lay in pools of their own waste. Rats scurried over their bodies. Sailors barked orders in a language the Africans couldn't understand. The prisoners soon learned to dread the crack of the lash. Slaves were flogged if they didn't exercise. They were flogged if they didn't obey orders. Even the sick were flogged to prevent malingering.

On the *Teçora* the Africans had plenty of food, but little water. Prisoners were whipped if they didn't eat—and some were forced to choke down so much that they vomited. As the days went by, the shackles cut into the slaves' wrists and legs, leaving sores that refused to heal. Diseases spread, and nearly one-third of the captives died at sea.

For about six weeks, the ship beat her way westward across the Atlantic. Then, toward the end of May, she headed into the Caribbean Sea.

The number of whippings suddenly decreased.

The slaves were given better food and were allowed to spend more time on deck. Some began to take heart, but Cinque and several others were uneasy. There had to be a reason for the crew's sudden burst of kindness, and they suspected that the *Teçora* might be nearing her destination.

CHAPTER 4

CUBA

On a night in early June, the *Teçora* prepared to make landfall.

The crew was tense as they approached the shores of Cuba, and with good reason.

Thirty-two years earlier, in 1807, the British outlawed the African slave trade and urged other countries to do the same. Many nations agreed and signed treaties that allowed British authorities to apprehend slave ships on the seas and enforce new antislave trade regulations. Spain was one of those nations.

In 1817, in exchange for a four-hundred-thousand-pound payment from Britain, the Spanish government instituted three important laws:

★ Spanish subjects could not bring newly captured African slaves to Spanish territory.
★ All Africans who had been shipped to Spanish territory *before 1820* would remain slaves.
★ All Africans who reached Spanish territory *after 1820* would be free.

The Spanish government—which made millions on sugar grown by Cuban slaves—didn't try to enforce those laws, but Great Britain did. Her fleet patrolled the Cuban coast, seized slave ships, arrested the crews, and freed newly imported Africans. Captains landed late at night in lonely places and some destroyed their ships after arriving to avoid detection. The penalty for violating the laws against the African slave trade was death, and the *Teçora*'s captain had to be careful.

Once the cargo was safely ashore, he could relax. Spanish officials on the island ignored the antislave trade laws. Approximately ten thousand illegally imported Africans—like Cinque—were sold in Cuban markets every year. Traders made huge profits, and government employees pocketed ten to seventeen dollars' worth of bribes on every sale.

It was dark when the *Teçora* finally reached the island. Sailors manned their posts. Below deck, the slaves waited as the captain eased the ship toward the shore and anchored near a tiny village. Crewmen promptly hustled the Africans ashore, chained them together, and marched them inland to a backwoods camp.

Ten or twelve days later, guards took the slaves on another nighttime trek. They stopped before dawn for a brief rest outside the massive walls of Havana, Cuba's capital city. Then, at sunrise, the slavers whisked their charges through the streets and deposited them in a large warehouse located near the governor's palace. The place looked like a roof-less barn and was used only for storing newly imported Africans. Cubans called it La Misericordia— the Spanish word for "mercy."

In the 1800s, many thought that captivity weakened slaves. Owners believed that native Africans were stronger than their American-born descendants, and customers from all over the West Indies came to La Misericordia to examine the most recent arrivals. Hard-eyed planters and traders regularly strolled through the compound looking for bargains. Overseers searched for fresh workers to replace the ones killed by poor food, beatings, and sixteen- to nineteen-and-a-half-hour workdays on coffee and sugar plantations. Merchants haggled. Tourists gaped at the half-naked "savages."

Toward the end of June, José Ruiz and Pedro Montes, two Spaniards from the Cuban town of Puerto Principe, paid a visit to the warehouse. Ruiz, a "gentlemanly" twenty-four-year-old slave dealer, had lived in the United States for a time and spoke fluent English. His gray-haired partner, fifty-eight-year-old Montes, had once been a sailor.

Montes bought four African children: three little girls and a boy, seven to ten years old.

Ruiz wanted strong young men. He spoke with the captain of the *Teçora* and then inspected the shipment. One by one, Ruiz singled out the likeliest candidates. He "made them open their mouths to see if their teeth were sound," prodded every part of their bodies, and inspected their private parts for signs of disease. As he ran his hands over Cinque's muscles, the Spaniard murmured, "Fine...fine." The *Teçora* slaves were of high quality, and Ruiz purchased Cinque, Grabeau, Burna, and forty-six other men for four hundred fifty dollars apiece. Then he and Montes went to the government offices.

There, for a bribe, Cuban officials prepared a

passport that would allow the two owners to take their new slaves safely through the British sea blockade. Since it was illegal to ship Africans across the ocean, the passport stated that the four children and the other men from the *Teçora* were *ladinos:* slaves who had been legally brought to Cuba before 1820, had lived on the island for the past nineteen years, and knew how to speak Spanish. To make the document look convincing, the two dealers gave each African a new Spanish name. Only one slave kept part of his original name. On the passport, Cinque was listed as Joseph Cinquez.

The document was ready on June 26. Two days later, the slaveowners returned to La Misericordia to pick up their purchases.

As Ruiz separated his merchandise from the rest of the *Teçora*'s cargo, women and children sobbed openly. Grabeau remained dry-eyed, stubbornly refusing to weep because he was "a man." But Cinque's eyes were full of tears.

Ruiz led his captives to the shore, where a ship was waiting. It was a sleek little schooner specially designed for carrying slaves. The name lettered on her shiny black hull was *L'Amistad*—the Spanish word for "friendship."

At eight P.M., Ruiz took his slaves aboard and

ordered them into the hold. Montes arrived about fifteen minutes later with the four children. The *Amistad*'s crew—two white sailors, a mulatto cook, and the captain's personal slave—stowed the rest of the cargo while the captain stood by.

By midnight, preparations were complete. Captain Ferrer gave the order to hoist anchor, and the schooner set out for Puerto Principe, roughly three hundred miles away.

CHAPTER 5

⟨⟩◆⟨⟩

"TRYING TO BE FREE"

It should have taken two days to reach Puerto Principe, but the winds were fickle, and after three days at sea the *Amistad* was still a long way from port. Slaves and crew sweltered in the fierce summer heat. Supplies ran low, and each African's total daily food ration was one banana, two potatoes, and a little cup of water.

Burna and several of the others were caught trying to steal a few extra sips from the ship's cask. Ruiz had them flogged, and the sailors rubbed a mixture of salt, rum, and gunpowder into their bleeding wounds to intensify the pain.

With gestures, Cinque asked the mulatto cook what would happen when the *Amistad* reached land.

The cook pointed to a barrel filled with beef. Using pantomime, he explained that when the ship docked, the slaves "would have their throats cut, be chopped into pieces, and salted down" to make meat for the Spaniards. It was a lie, but Cinque believed it and decided to act.

That afternoon he found a nail and hid it carefully under his arm.

In the evening, the Africans held a council to discuss the situation. "If we do nothing," Cinque said, "we [will] be killed. We may as well die in trying to be free...."

The others agreed, and Cinque outlined a plan.

On the night of July 1, a storm broke, and gusts of rain and wind battered the *Amistad*. While the crew fought to steady the ship, Cinque and Grabeau used the nail to detach the chain that connected the men's iron collars from its fitting in the wall. Once free, they began to search for weapons. One man found a case of sugarcane knives hidden among the boxes and barrels in the hold. The slaves armed themselves with the sharp two-foot-long machetes and sat down to wait.

As the evening wore on, the wind died down and

the rain slowed to a drizzle. Ruiz and Montes went to sleep in their quarters. The captain and crew dozed on the deck. The ship was quiet.

About four A.M., the freed slaves crept cautiously out of the hold. No one was standing guard. In the dim light, they could see the cook lying fast asleep in a rowboat. Cinque killed the man before he could raise the alarm and swiftly led his troops along the deck.

Minutes later, Captain Ferrer woke to find himself surrounded by slaves. Pulling his dagger, he charged the Africans, thrusting furiously. Ferrer killed one slave and wounded two others before he was cut down by a volley of blows. Noise wakened the slave-owners, and both Spaniards rushed on deck. Ruiz grabbed an oar and attacked the rebels. Montes lashed out with a knife and stick. "Kill them all," yelled one of the sailors, and the fight raged.

By dawn it was over. Cinque was in command of the ship.

CHAPTER 6

AT SEA

The *Amistad* was drifting in the ocean. None of the Africans knew how to sail it. The captain was dead. The two sailors had escaped in one of the ship's boats. Antonio, Captain Ferrer's former cabin boy and slave, was no seaman. The only people left on board who might know how to navigate were the two former slaveowners. With the help of Antonio, who spoke Spanish and a little Mende, Cinque ordered the Spaniards to take the helm and sail the ship to Africa.

Montes claimed he didn't know the way. But Cinque did. To reach Cuba, the *Teçora* had traveled toward the setting sun. Home, he reasoned, had to lie in the opposite direction.

Reluctantly, Montes took the wheel and followed orders. While he steered, Cinque watched; and at sunset the *Amistad* was on an eastward course.

At dawn, however, it was traveling in an entirely different direction. The Spaniard, it seemed, had turned the ship toward Cuba. Cinque quickly consulted his men. Then he picked up a knife and threatened the pilot. Montes dropped to his knees and begged for his life. After a few moments, Cinque let the old man go.

Shaken, Montes returned to the helm and turned the schooner eastward. But he hadn't given up.

Several days later, the two Spaniards wrote a distress message. They told Cinque it was a ticket to Africa and urged him to give it to the captain of a passing ship. The African accepted the letter politely, then tied it to a heavy piece of iron and dropped it in the sea.

Montes tried to signal other vessels until Cinque ordered the pilot to keep away from ships and settled areas. He also told the Africans to lock the Spaniards in the hold if any other craft approached.

Guards stationed at the helm kept a close watch on the pilot. Each day, while the sun shone, the

Spaniard steered east toward Africa, but at night he headed north toward the southern United States—where slavery was legal and the usual punishment for mutinous slaves was death.

For the whole month of July, the *Amistad* zigzagged over the Atlantic. Storms shredded her sails. The hot sun bleached her decks. Food stocks dwindled, and by August water supplies were dangerously low. Cinque rationed the last remaining gallons. After giving the largest shares to the children and Spaniards, he doled out small amounts to the others and took almost none himself. The allotment wasn't nearly enough, and some of the men tried to use seawater or medicine to quench their thirst.

Once Cinque had tried to avoid other ships. Now he let Burna hail passing vessels to ask for supplies. On August 18, the Africans bought some water from a passing schooner. Five days later, the captain of the *Eveline* gave them another cask of water and some apples. But when he offered to tow the *Amistad* to shore, Cinque abruptly raised sail. As August progressed, there were other encounters. Stories about a "long, low, black schooner" manned by a pirate crew filtered into the U.S. newspapers, and the U.S. Navy sent several ships to search for the mysterious stranger. But the *Amistad* sailed on.

Nearly two months had passed since the mutiny. Provisions were exhausted. Thirst, hunger, heat, and disease had weakened everyone. Ten men had already died, and many of the survivors were too sick to stand. When a lookout spied a lighthouse on a nearby stretch of coast, Cinque told Montes to head for land. On August 25, 1839, the *Amistad* finally dropped anchor in a quiet bay.

CHAPTER 7

LANDFALL

The first priority was finding food and water.
Cinque snatched some gold coins from the
Spaniards' strongbox to pay for supplies and
boarded the lifeboat. Grabeau, Burna, and several
others joined him, and together they rowed landward.

Once ashore, the Africans headed inland. A few
houses stood near the coast, and the *Amistad* group
went from one to another—trying to buy supplies.
Some residents wanted nothing to do with the
strange black men dressed in blankets. Others, however, sold the travelers potatoes, bread, gin, and two

dogs. No one stopped the Africans or threatened them; but one of the local residents, Captain Henry Green, decided to find out what these unusual visitors were up to. With four of his friends, Green went out to meet the Africans.

The two parties eyed each other. Using signs and a few English words, the *Amistad* group asked if there were slaves in this country.

Green and his friends answered no.

Were there Spaniards?

Again, the locals shook their heads.

The Africans let out a whoop and began to dance.

The *Amistad* had anchored off the coast of New York—and under New York State law Cinque and his companions were free!

But they still had to figure out how to get home.

Since Captain Green claimed to be a seaman, Cinque and Burna asked if he'd help them make the trip back to Africa. The American seemed interested. Negotiations began, and while the men were discussing terms the U.S. Coast Guard brig *Washington* sailed into the bay.

While cruising past the Long Island shoreline on a routine surveying mission, the brig's crew had spied the battered *Amistad* anchored by a lonely stretch of coast. The *Washington*'s commander, Lieutenant Thomas R. Gedney, thought it might be a smuggling ship and quickly ordered two officers to investigate the "strange and suspicious-looking vessel."

Minutes later, Lieutenant Richard W. Meade, Midshipman D. D. Porter, and six seamen armed with loaded muskets and pistols pulled alongside the schooner and swarmed up the rigging. On deck, they found the *Amistad*'s remaining crew: four small healthy children and a crowd of starved, half-naked men holding knives.

When Meade asked to see the ship's documents, the Africans stared helplessly. They didn't understand English. They were too weak to fight. Their knives were no match for the Americans' guns. There was nothing to do but surrender.

As the sailors were collecting the knives and herding their prisoners below at gunpoint, the two Spaniards raced on deck. Montes burst into tears, threw his arms around Porter, and shouted, "Bless the Holy Virgin, you are our preservers." Ruiz was more composed. In excellent English, he carefully thanked the two officers for rescuing them from a "ruthless gang" of mutinous slaves.

On the beach, Cinque and his men saw the *Washington,* jumped into their boat, and rowed furiously toward the *Amistad.* At the same time, Midshipman Porter and an armed crew left the schooner and headed toward the coast to find the landing party. Halfway between ship and shore, the two boats met.

Porter ordered Cinque's group to steer for the *Amistad,* but the men ignored the command and turned landward. The midshipman fired a warning shot and sped after them.

When the former slaves reached the coast, the *Washington*'s men were right behind them. Sailors quickly rounded up the Africans, forced them into the boats, and rowed back to the schooner.

After boarding the *Amistad,* Cinque went below with his followers. Then, before anyone could stop him, he dashed back onto the deck, ran to the rail, and leaped into the sea.

Meade sent a boat after him, but each time it came close the African dived and darted off in another direction. He dodged the Americans for almost an hour, but he couldn't escape, and the seamen finally hauled him into the gig. They took him to the *Washington,* but Cinque insisted on returning to the *Amistad.*

Once on board, he silenced the cheering Africans and then began to make a speech.

The Americans didn't know what Cinque was saying, but his words inflamed the crowd. Meade's men, fearing violence, abruptly grabbed the African leader, bundled him over the side, and took him to the *Washington.*

On the following day, Cinque persuaded the Americans to take him back to the schooner, where he delivered another rousing speech. As the former slaves started to yell and stamp, alarmed crewmen seized Cinque. They rowed him back to the *Washington,* put him in irons, and threw him in the brig.

As soon as all the Africans were safely under lock and key, Lieutenant Gedney towed the *Amistad* across Long Island Sound to Connecticut (one of the few Northern states where slavery was still legal). There, in the city of New London, he turned the ship and the prisoners over to federal officials.

On Friday, August 29, U.S. District Court Judge Andrew Judson boarded the *Washington* to conduct a brief investigation of the case. He examined the Cuban passport and listened to the Spaniards' testimony. Cinque, who was handcuffed and dressed in a red shirt and white trousers, watched the proceedings carefully. Since he knew no English, he could not tell his side of the story. Instead, he stared intently at Ruiz and Montes and "at intervals he motioned with his hand that he expected to be hanged." The African showed no fear, and one newspaper reporter thought he displayed "uncommon...coolness" and "a composure characteristic of true courage." The judge seemed less impressed. After a quick review of the evidence, he ordered the U.S. marshal to keep the Africans in prison until September 19, when a U.S. circuit court could decide whether the *Amistad* rebels should be charged with murder.

Two days later, the bewildered captives were taken from New London to the county jail in New Haven, Connecticut. Cinque was kept in chains and locked in a cell filled with common criminals. The other men and the children were shut into an apartment made up of four barracks-like rooms. Nearly one-third of the Africans were miserably sick with chronic diarrhea. Three were dying. They had no friends, no lawyers, and no money. They didn't know what the Americans planned to do with them. And they probably feared that the judge had already condemned them to death.

CHAPTER 8

—⟹◆⟸—

ENEMIES AND
FRIENDS

The *Amistad* story hit the newspapers at the end of August. By September, the Africans were famous—and Americans were arguing furiously about the merits of their case. Did Gedney have a legal right to arrest them? Should they be sent to Cuba? Shipped to Africa? Were they free men or mutinous slaves? Opinions clashed on every point, but that was not surprising. The central issue in the *Amistad* case was slavery, and slavery was the most controversial issue in the United States.

This conflict had been brewing since colonial times. The first black slaves reached Virginia in 1619.

Sixty-nine years later, Pennsylvania Quakers published the country's first antislavery pamphlet, and from that time until the end of the Civil War people quarreled over whether slavery should exist in a free country. Furious debates about the subject raged during the writing of the Declaration of Independence and the Constitution. Most Northern states banned the practice after the Revolutionary War. The Southern states retained it. Congress argued over whether to allow slavery in new states, and by the 1830s Americans were split into opposing groups.

Abolitionists—who thought slavery was a "wicked, fearful, bloody bargain"—helped runaway slaves, published antislavery newspapers, and urged the federal government to outlaw slavery in all states immediately. Pro-slavery activists fought back. They burned abolitionist pamphlets, tried to pass laws that protected the rights of slaveholders, and claimed that slavery was a "positive good" "instituted by God Himself." Other Americans disliked slavery but opposed abolitionists. They feared that immediate emancipation might damage the economy, create social unrest, and cause a split between the North and the South that would destroy the nation.

In 1831, a Virginia slave named Nat Turner organized and led a bloody rebellion that terrified white

Southerners, led to harsher slave laws, and helped to arouse anti-abolitionist sentiment. Gangs attacked abolitionists on city streets. Some politicians tried to avoid the dangerous subject, and in 1836, a coalition of Northern and Southern congressmen passed gag rules to prevent members from discussing anti-slavery petitions on the floor of the House of Representatives.

Slavery was on the nation's mind. It was on the nation's conscience, and the *Amistad*'s arrival fueled the great debate. Abolitionists and pro-slavery forces squared off over this new issue, and powerful men began to work for and against the prisoners.

Sympathetic Northern newspaper writers called Cinque a "hero."

In the South, a correspondent for the New Orleans *Times Picayune* dubbed him a "black piratical murderer."

"It is the duty of our government," trumpeted the Charleston *Mercury*, "to send these Negroes to Havana..." to receive the "punishment Spanish law inflicts for murder and rebellion."

The Spanish ambassador agreed. On September 6, he wrote a long letter to the U.S. secretary of state, explaining that the *Amistad* rebels had to be punished to prevent other slave revolts on the island of Cuba.

He pointed out that the U.S. government had signed a treaty in which it promised to return all Spanish slaves and other property rescued "from pirates or robbers on the high seas" to the proper Spanish owners. And he asked the U.S. government to send the prisoners to Cuba so that they could be tried for their crimes in Spanish courts.

President Martin Van Buren and his advisors considered the ambassador's request.

Van Buren had won the presidency because of Southern votes, and several of his cabinet officers came from slave states. Both he and his advisors thought that the United States should honor the treaty and stay on good terms with the powerful Spanish government.

Without bothering to find out whether Cinque and his companions were truly Spanish slaves, the Van Buren administration settled on a plan. They decided to have a U.S. government lawyer attend the September 19 circuit court session and ask the judge for permission to send the *Amistad* rebels back to Cuba.

At about the same time, Lewis Tappan and a group of other abolitionists decided to make sure that didn't happen.

Tappan, a wealthy New York businessman, devoted

much of his time and money to fighting slavery. He supported schools for African Americans, funded abolitionist newspapers, founded abolitionist societies—and discovered that being an abolitionist was dangerous. In 1834, a mob vandalized Tappan's house and burned his furniture. There were death threats in his mail, and one opponent offered a fifty-thousand-dollar reward for his corpse. Other men probably would have carried a gun for protection. Tappan simply tucked a copy of the New Testament in his pocket and went on with his work. When the *Amistad* arrived, he threw himself into the effort to help the captives.

With the help of several colleagues, Tappan organized the Committee for the Defense of the Africans of the *Amistad.* He sped up to New Haven to make sure Cinque and his companions were well treated and tried to stir up sympathy for the rebels by writing newspaper articles about them. Together the committee members raised money for the cause and tried to find the prisoners a lawyer.

New Haven attorney Roger Baldwin agreed to take the case. Baldwin, whose grandfather had signed the Declaration of Independence, was an excellent lawyer. He supported abolitionist causes and had successfully defended a runaway slave. He was willing to help the captives, but to do it he had to know their side of the story. That, however, was difficult because Baldwin couldn't understand most of what his clients said.

Burna knew only a few words of English. Antonio, who knew Spanish, didn't understand enough Mende to translate well, and none of the Americans knew what language the prisoners spoke or what part of Africa they came from.

Time was flying by. The September 19 circuit court hearing was only days away. The *Amistad* committee had to find an interpreter who could speak to the captives—and soon.

Professor Josiah Willard Gibbs, a language expert from Yale College,* thought of a plan. He visited the jail and, with signs, asked the Africans to count from one to ten. After memorizing the numbers, Gibbs hurried down to the docks to find an African sailor who could understand what *e-ta, fe-le, sau-wa, na-ni, do-lu, we-ta, waw-fe-la, wai-ya-gha, ta-u, pu* meant. But nobody recognized the words, and most people probably thought the professor was a little crazy.

Tappan searched too. After days of looking, the abolitionist finally located three English-speaking

* Yale College was renamed Yale University in 1887.

Africans who had recently come to the United States. He took all three to New Haven, hoping that at least one of them could communicate with the captives. Unfortunately, none of the would-be interpreters knew Mende—the language most of the prisoners spoke. Two of them couldn't understand the members of the *Amistad* group at all. The third, a man named John Ferry, managed to carry on a halting conversation with Grabeau and some of the others in Mandingo and Gallinao. Ferry didn't understand everything they said, but he was able to translate most of the story.

Tappan, Baldwin, and Ferry then went to interview Cinque.

At first, the prisoner was unwilling to talk. Then, slowly, he began to describe all that had happened since he and the others had left Africa five months ago.

Five months ago! That was important information. Spanish law stated that all Africans who reached Cuba after 1820 were free. If Baldwin could prove in court that the *Amistad* rebels had reached Cuba in 1839, the prisoners could not be treated as slaves. They could not be sent back to Cuba. And they could not be charged with murder, because free people had a legal right to fight to regain their liberty.

As quickly as possible, the Connecticut attorney began to prepare his arguments.

It was a challenging case. Some of the legal aspects of the defense were tricky, and there was a real chance that African defendants might not get a fair hearing.

In both the North and the South, racial prejudice was a basic part of American life. Many whites thought blacks belonged to an inferior race. Schools and churches were segregated. There were even some abolitionists who refused to associate with black people. In the North—where white workers and free blacks competed for the same jobs—tensions ran high. Bloody race riots erupted during the 1830s, and white mobs attacked African Americans on the streets of Hartford, Philadelphia, Pittsburgh, and other cities.

Slaves had no legal rights. Even free blacks did not have the same rights as other Americans. In most places, only white men could vote, testify in court, or serve on juries. It was hard to defend black men, but Baldwin was hopeful.

In the New Haven jail, however, the prisoners had little to cheer about. Three more of them died in the first two weeks of September, and a local doctor was called frequently to take care of others who were sick.

In public, the captives were quiet and polite. Most, however, must have been uncomfortable in their new surroundings. They weren't used to American weather, American customs, American food—and American clothes were a new experience. At home in the tropics, the Africans wore little, but in chilly New Haven they had to dress warmly. When the jailers handed out garments, the little girls slid into their first calico dresses and twisted their new shawls into turbans. The men just burst out laughing when they tried to put on their stiff cotton shirts and dark striped trousers.

Americans were fascinated by the captives. They wanted to know more about Cinque. They wondered if Konnoma—the captive with pointed fanglike teeth—was a cannibal. (He wasn't.) Most of all, they wanted to see what the celebrities looked like. Huge crowds milled around the prison, hoping for a glimpse of the famous Africans. Peddlers sold pictures of Cinque in the city streets; and the chief jailer, Colonel Pendleton, set up his own ticket concession. He charged sightseers twelve and a half cents a look, and in a few days nearly four thousand visitors paid to gape at the rebels.

For the prisoners, every week was full of staring eyes and disturbing events. The Africans were afraid that the grave, black-clad clergyman who visited the jail were executioners or judges. When a military parade went past, they wanted to know if the marching soldiers were coming to "cut their throats." With the help of John Ferry, the interpreter, Tappan and others tried to tell the captives that they hadn't been sentenced to death. But the Africans didn't seem to believe it.

On September 14, when the group boarded the canal boat that would take them to Hartford, Connecticut, for the circuit court hearing, the children cried. The men looked drawn and tense. Every one of them clearly expected the worst.

CHAPTER 9

---◈---

THE CIRCUIT COURT HEARING

Hartford was buzzing with excitement. For days, people from nearby towns and faraway cities such as New York and Boston had been streaming into Connecticut's capital. Hotels were packed. Crowds swarmed through the streets. By September 19, the city was bursting with visitors who wanted to see the captives and attend the hearing (a court session in which lawyers present evidence to a judge, who decides the case).

One man traveled a hundred miles just to find out what real live Africans looked like. Tourists cheerfully asked one another for directions to the jail, and a flood of sightseers poured inside to gawk at the prisoners.

The defendants thought the mob had come to see them hanged. "If they don't mean to kill us," they asked, "why are so many people here...?" John Ferry tried to reassure them, and they waited uneasily in their prison quarters for the legal proceedings to begin.

The courtroom was jammed on the first day of the session. Spectators jostled for seats, and everyone suddenly turned to stare when a guard brought the little girls into the chamber. Terrified, the children clutched the jailer's hands and began to cry. The man tried to pacify them with pieces of fruit, but the youngsters ignored the sweets and sobbed miserably.

At the front of the room, a flock of attorneys fussed over their papers. Ruiz and Montes had hired two lawyers to represent their interests. U.S. District Attorney William Holabird was there to present the views of the Van Buren administration. Roger Baldwin and a team of assistants had come to defend the prisoners. Late in the afternoon, Judge Smith Thompson finally opened the proceedings, and the battle began.

Ruiz and Montes's lawyers asked the judge to return the "slaves" to their clients.

District Attorney Holabird objected. He explained that the Spanish government claimed jurisdiction under the terms of a treaty and wanted the prisoners sent to Havana so that Spanish courts could decide whether they were criminals or slaves.

No, retorted Roger Baldwin. Spanish authorities had no right to claim the prisoners because Cinque and his companions were *not* Spanish. The prisoners were native Africans, Baldwin told the court. They had been brought to Cuba nineteen years after Spain had banned the slave trade in 1820. Under Spanish law, the defendants were not slaves!

But were they criminals? Baldwin asked. Was their mutiny a crime? No, cried the defense attorney, the Africans did what "every one of us would have done, if placed in similar circumstances." They fought for liberty.

Cinque and his companions were legally free when they arrived in Cuba. They were legally free when they sailed on the *Amistad*. They were free when Lieutenant Gedney found them. And, thundered Baldwin, "I say there is no power on earth that has a right...to reduce them to slavery."

The lawyers argued for two and a half days, till, at seven o'clock Saturday night, the hearing ended. Alone, Thompson thoughtfully reviewed the arguments. Personally, he detested slavery. He sympathized with the prisoners, but he couldn't let personal feelings influence the decision. Judges had to obey the law—and that was exactly what Smith Thompson planned to do.

On Monday morning, September 23, the courtroom again was packed.

In an earlier session, Thompson had ruled that the *Amistad* rebels could not be tried for murder in the United States, because the mutiny had not occurred in U.S. territory. Under U.S. law, Cinque and his companions were *not* criminals. But what were they, then? Slaves who ought to be shipped back to Cuba? Or free Africans who ought to be sent home?

As the crowd listened intently, Smith Thompson explained that as a *circuit court* judge, he did not have the power to answer that question. U.S. law stated that slaves were "property," and property disputes had to be settled in *district courts*. Legally, there was only one thing the judge could do. Although the decision was "painful," Judge Thompson ruled that the rebels would have to stay in jail—for safekeeping—until a U.S. district court could decide whether they were free men or slaves.

That hearing would take place on January 7, 1840—almost four months away.

CHAPTER 10

———⟫◆⟪———

PLANS AND
PREPARATIONS

Cinque and the other Africans settled back into their quarters at the New Haven jail. They were still prisoners, but—thanks to the court's decision—officials no longer treated them like criminals.

After the hearing, jailers removed Cinque's chains. They allowed him to live with the other men, and on the trip back to New Haven they let him sit outside with the stagecoach driver. Once, during a short stop, the coachman tossed Cinque the reins. For a few moments, said a reporter, the African sat alone in the fresh air, holding the horses—just as if he were a free man.

But of course he wasn't free. Both he and his companions still had to prove they were not slaves at the January district court hearing—and that was several months away. In the meantime, the captives needed to talk to their lawyers and jailers—and to do that they had to learn English.

Tappan helped organize the lessons. Students and professors from nearby Yale College offered to teach. Each day, for two to five hours, part of the New Haven jail became a classroom and the Africans went to school.

At first, the work was simple. Teachers held up a picture of an object, named it, and asked the students to repeat the word. Later, Cinque and the others also learned to read and write in English. They studied the Bible as well. Tappan and his colleagues hoped the Africans would eventually become Christians, so religious instruction was an important part of the program.

The prisoners were "quick, shrewd...intelligent" pupils. Most seemed to like the lessons, and they begged instructors to come early and stay late. Good students helped slower ones, but learning the new language wasn't easy. Although John Ferry did his best, he couldn't always translate the students' questions or the teachers' explanations properly. The

Africans desperately needed a better interpreter.

Fortunately, after weeks of searching for someone who could understand the Mende numbers he had learned, Professor Gibbs finally hit the jackpot. On the New York waterfront, he met James Covey, a young black sailor serving aboard the British warship *Buzzard*. Like most of the prisoners in the New Haven jail, Covey was Mende. He'd been kidnapped by slavers as a child, rescued from a slave ship by the British, and raised in a British colony near Mende territory. Covey spoke both English and Mende fluently, and he was willing to help. His captain gave him permission to leave the ship, and Gibbs rushed him to New Haven.

The prisoners were eating breakfast when the new interpreter arrived. A guard refused to let him enter the dining room, but one of the Africans heard voices and got up to find out what the fuss was about. He heard Covey speak a few words of Mende and instantly pulled the newcomer into the room. Excited Africans crowded around the stranger, laughing, clapping, and "talking as fast as possible." With Covey's help, they could finally tell Americans the whole story.

As the trees outside the New Haven jail turned to fiery reds and golds, Baldwin and the other defense lawyers continued to work on the case.

In New York, Tappan was busy raising money for the prisoners' expenses and writing newspaper articles to drum up support for their cause.

Americans were obsessed with the *Amistad* affair. It was, said a reporter, the most exciting "event that has occurred since the close of the last century. The parsons preach about [the Africans]," he said, "the men talk about them, [and] the ladies give tea parties and discuss [them]." A play entitled "The Black Schooner, or the Pirate Slaver *Amistad*" opened at New York's Bowery Theater. Wax museums displayed figures of the rebels, and William Cullen Bryant, one of America's best-known writers, published a dramatic poem that described Cinque as a "warrior true and brave." Articles about the mutiny even appeared in foreign newspapers; in Cuba, Dr. Richard Madden read about the case.

Madden, an Irish-born abolitionist, had spent the last three years in Havana, serving on a British government commission charged with stamping out the illegal Cuban slave trade. He knew how traders smuggled Africans in and out of the country, and he thought his knowledge might help the *Amistad* captives.

With his own money, Madden bought a ticket to

New York. In early November, he met Tappan and talked to the prisoners. Then he offered to testify for the defense.

The district court hearing was scheduled for January, but Madden couldn't stay in the United States that long. Lawyers quickly contacted the judge, and a special session was arranged. On November 20, the *Amistad* attorneys met in the chambers of District Court Judge Andrew Judson—the same man who had jailed the mutineers in August—to hear Madden's testimony.

Under oath, the British abolitionist swore that the prisoners' "language, appearance, and manners" showed that they had "been very recently brought from Africa." He said that the Cuban passport was clearly a fraud. In his expert opinion, Madden declared, the *Amistad* rebels could not possibly be Spanish slaves.

It was powerful testimony, and Baldwin planned to present it at the January 7 district court hearing.

December passed, and in January bitter winter weather gripped the Northeast. Rivers froze, harbors were clogged with ice, and snow blanketed New England. Dressed in heavy clothes and shoes, Cinque and his friends huddled beside the glowing prison stove. There were fewer of them now. Some had never recovered from the terrible trip on the *Amistad.* Three more of the men had died since October. Although most of the group was alive and well, the long months of hardship had taken a toll. One of the men cried every day, and sometimes the Africans must have wondered if they would ever be free.

Miles away in Washington, the president and his advisors were also worried about the progress of the *Amistad* affair. The Spanish ambassador kept demanding "delivery" of the "assassins." Many Southerners supported the Spanish claim, and Van Buren needed Southern votes to win a second term in the 1840 presidential election. The case was a problem, but the Van Buren administration thought of a way to solve it once and for all.

Judge Judson was known for his racist views, and the Van Buren administration assumed he'd decide that the rebels were slaves. As soon as Judson made the expected decision, the president and his cabinet planned to have federal officials seize the Africans, put them aboard a navy ship, and whisk them off to Cuba—before the prisoners' lawyers had a chance to object.

Under United States law, a person who is dissatisfied with the outcome of a hearing or trial has the right to file an appeal asking a higher court to review his case and change the decision. Sending the prisoners to Cuba would deprive them of that basic right. But that didn't seem to bother Van Buren and his men.

On January 2, the secretary of the navy sent a top-secret letter to Lieutenant John S. Paine, commander of the navy schooner *Grampus*. It ordered Paine to sail to New Haven, wait for the district court decision, and then carry out the administration's plan.

Dismayed, Paine wrote back to say that sailing from New Haven to Cuba in January was dangerous and that his ship was too small to house his crew and all the prisoners. Unless the secretary allowed the *Grampus* to sail with fewer hands, the Africans would have to stay on deck in the freezing cold.

The secretary agreed to let Paine reduce his crew and ordered the lieutenant to get on with the operation. Paine had to obey, and the *Grampus* set sail for New Haven on her "special and delicate" mission.

CHAPTER 11

THE DISTRICT COURT HEARING

On Tuesday, January 7, 1840, classes at Yale Law School were canceled so students could attend the district court hearing. By early morning, a mob of students, professors, dignitaries, reporters, and townspeople had filled every seat in the New Haven courtroom.

Judge Andrew Judson opened the hearing, and the defense team took the floor. With carefully prepared arguments, Roger Baldwin and his assistants demonstrated that the Africans could not be Spanish slaves, because they'd been taken to Cuba after Spain had banned the slave trade in 1820. One after another, their witnesses hammered home the most important points.

Dwight Janes, who had met the Spaniards soon after the *Amistad* docked in Connecticut, told the court he'd heard Ruiz say that Cinque and his companions were "just from Africa."

Interpreter James Covey said that in his opinion the prisoners had left Africa a very short time ago.

Professor Gibbs stated that, after analyzing the prisoners' "language and manners," he had "formed a decided opinion that they are native Africans and recently from Africa."

Defense attorneys read the testimony Dr. Madden had given earlier, and on January 8, Baldwin called his star witness.

With his head high and a blanket draped around his shoulders, Cinque marched to the stand, took the oath, and began to tell his story. Crouching, he showed how the slaves had been chained and packed into the *Teçora*'s hold. He described their sale to Ruiz and Montes in Havana, the starvation and beatings aboard the *Amistad,* and, finally, the way he and his companions had mutinied and traveled across the sea in search of freedom. He spoke in Mende. Covey translated. But once, in English, Cinque cried out, "Give us free! Give us free!" Spectators were spellbound. A reporter for the New Haven *Herald* was impressed by the witness's "sagacity...keenness and decision."

The defense had clearly shown that the prisoners were native Africans, but U.S. Attorney Holabird offered evidence that indicated the captives were truly Spanish slaves.

First, the U.S. attorney displayed the passport signed by the captain general of Cuba, which stated that the *Amistad* Africans were slaves who had been brought to Cuba legally before 1820.

Then Mr. Holabird read the court a statement written by Antonio Vega, a Spanish government official. In his remarks, Señor Vega said that the Cuban passport was "genuine." He also claimed that there was "no law...in force in the island of Cuba that prohibited the bringing in of African slaves."

On January 10, Lieutenant Paine anchored off the Connecticut coast to wait for the decision. In the courtroom, the attorneys battled over legal points and presented their closing arguments.

After Holabird delivered his summation, it was Baldwin's turn.

"Now," said the defense attorney, "I ask: Are these men property?"

No, he declared. No one had proved that Cinque

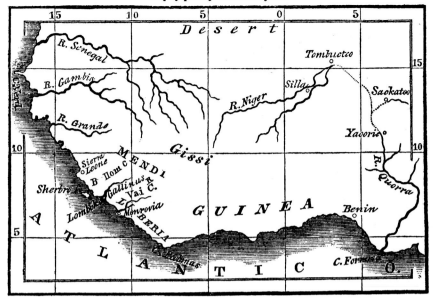

Map of part of Western Africa.

Map and artist's conception of Cinque's homeland from *A History of the* Amistad *Captives,* by John W. Barber, published in 1840. (New Haven Colony Historical Society)

Village in Mendi, with Palm trees, &c.

3 feet 3 in. high

Artists' conceptions of conditions aboard the slave ship *Teçora* (top), and of the *Amistad* mutiny (bottom) from *A History of the* Amistad *Captives.* (New Haven Colony Historical Society)

Death of Capt. Ferrer, the Captain of the Amistad, July, 1839

Painting showing the USS *Washington* (far left) and the *Amistad* (center) off Culloden Point, Long Island, 1839. In the lower right-hand corner, Cinque's landing party is shown coming ashore to trade. (New Haven Colony Historical Society)

Cinque, leader of the *Amistad* revolt. Watercolor portrait by
Nathaniel Jocelyn, *c.* 1840. The painter was the brother of a
member of the *Amistad* committee and an abolitionist in his
own right. His house became a stop on the Underground
Railway, the secret escape route for runaway slaves. (New
Haven Colony Historical Society)

Painting of John Quincy Adams (left), the former president who argued the *Amistad* case before the Supreme Court. (Library of Congress)
Roger S. Baldwin (right), principal lawyer for the *Amistad* captives. Engraving by A. H. Ritchie, based on a daguerreotype. (Baldwin Family Papers, Yale University Library)

Oil-on-canvas sketches for a series of murals created for Talladega College by Hale Woodruff, *c.* 1940. From top to bottom, the panels show the mutiny on the *Amistad,* José Ruiz pointing an accusing finger at Cinque in court, and the captives' return to Africa. (New Haven Colony Historical Society)

and his friends were ever "legally and truly" slaves. But, cried Baldwin, "evidence before this court has...established that they are and ought to be as God left them at their birth—FREE and INDEPEN-DENT!"

Baldwin spoke for four hours, and after more legal maneuvering the hearing ended on Saturday, January 11. Now, the judge had to make the final decision.

On Monday, January 13, Andrew Judson entered the courtroom, faced the waiting crowd, and announced that Cinque and his companions were "born free and still...are free and not slaves."

The Africans had won.

The delighted prisoners "leaped from their seats" when *Amistad* committee members brought them the news.

Cinque gripped Baldwin's hand. "We thank you," he said, "we bless you, this is all we can do for you."

The New York *Commercial Advertiser* called Judson's decision "lucid, able, and most righteous."

The Spanish ambassador said it was "scandalous."

Lieutenant Paine quickly sailed his ship away from the Connecticut coast. The *Grampus*'s mission was over, but the excitement was not.

The president and his advisors still wanted to hand

the prisoners over to Spanish authorities—and there was only one legal way to do it.

In April 1840, the Van Buren administration asked the U.S. Supreme Court—the highest court in the land—to review the *Amistad* case and overturn Judge Judson's decision.

U.S. Attorney Holabird filed the necessary papers for the appeal—and the celebrating stopped. The Africans would have to stay in jail while they waited for the Court to decide whether they were free people or Spanish slaves.

CHAPTER 12

———⊱◈⊰———

"GOD WILLING, WE WILL MAKE YOU FREE"

For the first time, the Africans seemed to lose heart. Teachers came, but none of the prisoners felt like working on their lessons. They couldn't see much point in learning English now. For a few days after hearing about the Supreme Court appeal, they ignored their books. Then—perhaps because studying was a good distraction—they went back to school. The teachers were pleased with the progress, but their pupils weren't happy.

During 1840, the old New Haven jail was torn down and the group was moved to cramped, uncomfortable quarters in the nearby town of Westville.

The three girls lived in the home of Colonel Pendleton, the warden, but all thirty-five men and the boy, Kali, had to share a single thirty-by-twenty-foot room. A visitor thought the clothing and bedding supplies were inadequate, and Cinque told Baldwin that Pendleton sometimes chained or whipped his people.

For the most part, the prisoners kept their feelings to themselves. After the warden told them that their bursts of anger frightened white people, Cinque and his friends tried to hide their emotions. They laughed and chatted politely with visitors; but, one of them admitted, they were homesick, and worried.

No other U.S. court could change a Supreme Court decision. If the Court found that the Africans were slaves, Cinque and his friends would be handed over to Spanish officials, shipped to Cuba, and probably sentenced to be hanged or burned to death. And there was a real chance that might happen.

Five of the nine Supreme Court justices were Southerners who had once owned slaves. They probably wouldn't sympathize with a band of black mutineers, and all five could easily vote against the prisoners.

Tappan and his colleagues tried to think of some way to improve the odds. They knew that Roger Baldwin was a skillful lawyer, but he wasn't well-known, and the justices might be more impressed by a famous attorney. But who?

It had to be someone with a national reputation, someone who could sway the Court, someone who was not afraid to represent blacks or speak out publicly against slavery.

Tappan asked the distinguished New England trial lawyer Rufus Choate to represent the prisoners, but Choate refused to take the case.

U.S. Senator Daniel Webster, a famous attorney and orator, also declined. There was, however, one other possibility.

On October 27, 1840, Lewis Tappan and abolitionist Ellis Gray Loring knocked at the door of a fine old house in the Massachusetts countryside. They had come to ask former United States President John Quincy Adams to represent the *Amistad* captives before the Supreme Court.

Adams, the son of the second president of the United States, had served as a U.S. ambassador, senator, secretary of state, and president. He had negotiated important treaties, traveled all over Europe, and somehow managed to find time to read books in five languages, keep up an enormous correspondence, and make detailed daily entries in his diary. At sixty-four, he ran for Congress; and now, at age seventy-three, he was still working full-time as a member of the U.S. House of Representatives. Tough, stubborn, and fiercely independent, Adams did what he thought was right, no matter what the cost. He hated slavery. He believed the *Amistad* prisoners should be freed. Yet when Tappan and Loring asked him to take the case, the old man said no. And for good reason.

His eyesight was failing. His hands sometimes trembled. Congressional duties already took up most of his time. Besides, he hadn't argued a law case in almost thirty years. At this point in life, Adams explained, he simply wasn't the right person for the job.

The two visitors begged the former president to reconsider. The hearing, they pointed out, was a matter of "life and death."

Adams hesitated. Then, finally, he said, "By the blessing of God, I will argue the case before the Supreme Court."

The abolitionists were delighted. Adams's family was not. Relatives hoped that he would drop the case before it damaged his health, his reputation, and their peace of mind. They were afraid he'd receive death threats and hate mail from forces opposed to black people and abolitionism. They even feared that public outcry might prevent Adams's son from being elected to the Massachusetts House of Representatives. But family protests had no effect. John Quincy Adams had made up his mind.

On November 17, the elderly gentleman bustled down to New Haven to confer with Roger Baldwin, who would be presenting part of the argument at the Supreme Court hearing. The two lawyers discussed the case at length and then drove out to Westville. There the former president was introduced to his new clients. As he shook hands with Cinque and Grabeau, the former president said, "God willing, we will make you free."

CHAPTER 13

―※◆※―

"CERTAIN INALIENABLE RIGHTS"

In February 1840, journalists found out about the Van Buren administration's attempt to ship the prisoners to Cuba on the *Grampus*. When newspapers printed the story, shocked Americans learned that the president had been willing to break the law, interfere with the courts, and deprive prisoners of their most basic legal rights.

Nine months later, voters turned Van Buren out of office and elected William Henry Harrison the ninth president of the United States. Harrison, however, would not begin his term until March 4,* 1841.

In the meantime, Martin Van Buren remained in power.

The Spanish ambassador continued to demand that the U.S. government send the *Amistad* prisoners back to Cuba.

The case remained on the Supreme Court agenda. Some abolitionists worried about the outcome of the Supreme Court hearing. A friend of Tappan's thought it might be a good idea to kidnap the Africans and take them to a safe place before the Court even considered the case.

Christmas passed, and another year began. The hearing was scheduled to begin soon, and in Westville Cinque and his companions waited anxiously. They couldn't help plan the legal strategy or argue the case, but two of them did try to tell their new attorney how they felt.

Kinna, one of the best English students, sent a letter asking the former president "to tell [the] court let Mendi people be free."

Another named Kale wrote:

* Today, the president is inaugurated on January 20. Before 1934, however, inauguration day was March 4.

Dear Friend Mr. Adams,

    I want to write a letter to you because you love Mendi people and you talk to the Great Court. We want to tell you one thing. Jose Ruiz say we born in [Havana], he tell lie...we all born in Mendi.... Every day and night we think about our country.... We want you to tell court that Mendi people no want to go back to Havana. We no want to be killed.... All we want is make us free....

In Washington, D.C., Adams was trying to do just that. At night, the lamps in his study burned late as he painstakingly studied stacks of documents to prepare for the hearing. The case was complex. Adams's legal skills were rusty, and nothing seemed to go right. His wife became ill. His thoughts seemed muddled, and a painful eye infection temporarily left him half-blind and unable to read. Many people thought that the prisoners didn't have much of a chance, and the old man was afraid of failing. "With deep anguish of heart," he searched for the best way to "expose" the U.S. government's "abominable conspiracy against the lives of these wretched men." In his diary he wrote, "Oh! how shall I do justice to this case and these men?"

The hearing was delayed and then delayed again. Finally, on February 22, George Washington's birthday, the United States Supreme Court met to consider the *Amistad* case.

The tiny semicircular courtroom beneath the Senate chamber in the Capitol building was crammed with lawyers and spectators. Adams and Baldwin appeared for the defendants. Attorney General Henry Gilpin was ready to represent the United States government. And up on the high mahogany bench, in solemn black robes, sat the Supreme Court justices. One justice was ill, so only eight were present. Four were from the South, four from the North, and a majority vote would decide the case. Chief Justice Roger Taney, a Southerner, opened the proceedings in case 2310: *The United States vs. The Libellants & Claimants of the Schooner* Amistad *and the Africans mentioned in the General Libels and Claims.*

At a Supreme Court hearing, lawyers present their arguments and answer questions from the justices. Attorneys today must state their position in a few minutes. In 1841, however, there was no time limit. Lawyers spoke for hours, and listeners who had followed the earlier *Amistad* hearings must have found the arguments familiar.

Attorney General Gilpin argued that the rebels had to be surrendered to Spanish authorities because of the treaty between the United States and Spain. He told the Court that the Cuban passport said that Cinque and his companions were slaves, and claimed that U.S. courts had no right to question the statements on this official Spanish document.

Roger Baldwin responded. In a brilliant day-and-a-half-long speech, he showed that the Cuban passport was a fraud and asserted that the Africans were free men under both United States and Spanish law.

While Baldwin spoke, Adams reviewed his own arguments. Despite all the preparation, he still didn't know exactly what he wanted to say. As soon as Baldwin's speech ended, the old man hurried over to the Library of Congress to do some last-minute research and then walked home through the winter gloom.

The following morning, Adams was almost sick with worry. He worked on his text until the last possible moment and entered the Supreme Court chamber with a sinking heart.

The room was packed. John Quincy Adams was one of the greatest orators of the day. Admirers called him Old Man Eloquent, and people from all over the city had come to hear him speak.

Chief Justice Taney asked the former president to begin. As Adams rose to face the bench, his nervousness suddenly melted away and his words rang through the courtroom.

He had come, Adams explained, to ask the Court to grant justice to thirty-six people who had been *un*justly enslaved by the Spanish, *un*justly captured by the United States Coast Guard, and *un*justly treated by the United States government.

Since when, he asked, did members of an administration have the right to substitute "sympathy with the white [and] antipathy to the black" for justice?

What right did Martin Van Buren—or any U.S. president—have to break the law, ignore the courts, and illegally order a United States naval vessel to take innocent human beings "to Cuba, to be sold...to be put to death, to be burned at the stake...?"

Did the Declaration of Independence justify slavery? "That DECLARATION," the former president reminded the Court, "says that every man is 'endowed by his Creator with certain inalienable rights,' and that 'among these are life, liberty, and the pursuit of happiness.'" Pointing dramatically to a framed copy of the document on the courtroom wall, Adams cried, "The moment you come to the Declaration of Independence...this case is decided. I ask nothing more on behalf of these unfortunate men than this Declaration."

The former president spoke for four and a half hours that day. When the session opened on the following morning, the chief justice announced that Justice Barbour of Virginia—one of the justices who was hearing the case—had died suddenly and that the Court would adjourn for several days. When the proceedings reopened on March 1, Adams spoke for three more hours and finished his address.

An article in the *Log Cabin* said that the speech "surpassed the most raised expectations in regard to its interest and power." The New York *Commercial Advertiser* noted, however, that some people didn't think it was "a good legal speech." Adams himself was dissatisfied, but it was too late to make changes. Now all he—and the defendants—could do was hope.

On March 9, the day scheduled for the ruling, Adams reached the court early and waited anxiously until the session opened. At last, the justices filed in. All eyes were fixed on the bench as Mr. Justice Story announced that the prosecution had not proved that Cinque and the other rebels were ever legally Spanish slaves. Therefore, Story said, under "the eternal principles of justice, and international law," the Africans were free.

"With great haste and great joy," Adams sent out the news.

The prisoners were waiting together when U.S. Marshal Willcox burst in to announce, "The big Court has come to a decision. They say that you—one and all—are free."

"[I am] glad," Cinque replied. "[I] thank the American men."

Others were also grateful. On March 13, 1841, *The Colored American,* one of the first U.S. newspapers published and edited by African Americans, printed a headline that read, "*Amistad* Captives—Victory—Justice Triumphant." Underneath, the paper printed an article that ended with the words "May we thank God and take courage."

Law had triumphed over politics, justice over prejudice. At a time when most African Americans had no legal rights, the *Amistad* captives had done what most blacks thought was impossible. They had fought for liberty and equal justice in United States courts and won.

CHAPTER 14

"I Am Very Glad This Day"

Now all the Africans wanted was to go home. America was a "good country," Cinque explained, but it wasn't theirs. Fuli summed up everyone's feelings: "If [American] men offer me...gold...and give me houses, land and every-[thing] so [that] I stay in this country, I say NO!... I want to see my father, my mother, my brother and sister."

Before making arrangements for the trip to Africa, however, the *Amistad* committee had to take care of two other important matters.

The first was Antonio. Since Antonio had been

born in Cuba, the Supreme Court had decided that the former cabin boy was legally a slave and had to be returned to his Cuban owners. Lewis Tappan, however, refused to let that happen. He smuggled the young man out of the country, and by the end of April Antonio was safe—and free—in Canada.

That done, the *Amistad* committee turned to the next task: finding safe temporary quarters for Cinque and the other newly released prisoners. Fortunately, Tappan knew just the place: Farmington, a small Connecticut village that housed two antislavery societies and would soon become an important stop on the Underground Railway.

In Farmington, the three little girls, Teme, Kagne, and Margru, boarded with local families while the men lived together in a barn that had been converted into lodgings. Several of their old teachers continued to give lessons, and the group settled into a routine. During the day, they studied reading, spelling, the Bible, and arithmetic—which was one of their favorite subjects. They grew vegetables in their own garden, shopped, took long walks, and made friends with many of their neighbors. Children were especially fond of the visitors, and Cinque sometimes turned somersaults and handsprings to entertain the local boys and girls.

While most townspeople welcomed the former captives, not everyone in Farmington was hospitable. A few residents objected to having "cannibals" in the neighborhood, and one day a band of bullies deliberately knocked Grabeau into a ditch. Cinque came to his rescue and fought off the thugs. It was a nasty incident.

The *Amistad* committee wanted to send the Africans home before there was more unpleasantness. But none of the Americans knew exactly where "home" was. Mende Land didn't appear on standard maps. It wasn't mentioned in American geography books, and the former prisoners couldn't provide precise directions. Tappan and his colleagues asked missionaries and colonial officials in Africa for information. Letters traveled back and forth across the ocean, and finally the British governor of Sierra Leone wrote to say that Mende Land was near his territory.

Now the *Amistad* committee had to raise money for the trip. Tappan published an appeal in the newspapers, and contributions began to roll in. Ten dollars came from a clergyman's widow. A Vermont farmer sent five. Some donated only a few pennies; but in the 1840s, when male factory workers earned about eight dollars and fifty cents a week, that was often a substantial gift.

The donations, however, weren't enough. To make up the shortfall, the committee decided to organize a fund-raising tour.

While most of the group stayed in Farmington, Cinque, Kale, Kinna, six other men, and little Margru put on their best clothes and began to travel. On railroads, in carriages, on steamboats, they journeyed through Massachusetts, Pennsylvania, Connecticut, New Hampshire, and New York, sometimes doing two "shows" a day at meeting halls and churches.

People crowded in to hear members of the troupe read aloud from the Bible and sing a variety of hymns and African songs. One of the men told the story of their adventures in English, and Cinque thrilled listeners with a dramatic account of the mutiny in Mende. After each performance, the company shook hands with members of the audience, sold napkins and tablecloths they'd made, and answered questions. In one place, a spectator asked Kinna, "Do American men believe in the Bible?" "Yes," he replied, "abolitionists."

Many Americans welcomed the "Mendian" travelers. When the group visited a Massachusetts rug factory, workers promptly took up a collection and donated $58.50 to the *Amistad* fund. In

Northampton, Massachusetts, Cinque and his friends stayed in the best rooms in the best hotel for free. But in Hartford, Connecticut, a hotel manager refused to give them rooms at any price. When hecklers taunted the troupe in the streets of Springfield, Massachusetts, Kinna told the audience about the incident. "We said nothing to them," he explained. "Why did they treat us so?"

After two long years of waiting, home was still only a dream, and by summer some of the Africans seemed to be losing hope.

One night, as the pale, beautiful lights of the aurora borealis shimmered in the New England sky, fourteen-year-old Teme told her guardian, "I think we never see Mendi any more."

Fone began to brood. When friends asked what was wrong, the young man said he was thinking of his mother. In August, he drowned while swimming in the Farmington canal. No one was sure whether it was an accident or a suicide.

As the months dragged by, the men began to skip lessons and ignore their teachers. Fortunately, preparations were almost complete. By fall 1841, the *Amistad* committee had collected enough money for fares and had assembled a group of missionaries who would accompany the Africans home and then set up a Christian church and school in Mende Land.

At five o'clock one chilly November morning, Cinque, Grabeau, and the others gathered their belongings and went to the Farmington dock to board the chartered canal boat that would take them to New York on the first leg of their journey. Despite the hour, the wharf was crowded. Nearly one hundred Farmington citizens had come to say good-bye. In a flurry of handshakes, tears, and good wishes, the former prisoners climbed aboard. Slowly, the craft pulled away, and in a few minutes the town and the waving crowd had vanished behind the rolling Connecticut hills.

When they reached New York, there were dozens of last-minute preparations, more farewells, and a final public appearance to raise money for the *Amistad* committee's Mende mission. With Tappan's help, the Africans also sent an inscribed copy of the Bible to John Quincy Adams as a thank-you gift. Adams, touched, wrote back: "My friends,...I...shall keep it as a kind remembrance from you to the end of my life.... May the Almighty Power which has preserved and sustained you hitherto, still go with you."

The days flew by, and finally, on November 27, 1841, after two years and three months in the United States, the former slaves said one last good-bye to

Lewis Tappan and boarded the ship that would take them home.

Cinque and the others kept a close eye on the ship's navigation, but they needn't have worried. This captain was an honest man. He steered east, toward the rising sun, and after a seven-week voyage, they were close to the African coast.

When the great lion-shaped mountains of Sierra Leone suddenly rose over the horizon, the former captives laughed and sang. As the ship sped toward the green palm-fringed coast, the missionaries heard the Africans murmur, *"Nya go-hung ni-engo ha"*—"I am very glad this day." After a long and perilous journey, Cinque and his companions had come home.

EPILOGUE

After the *Amistad* captives returned to Africa, many of the people described in this book settled back into their old lives and disappeared from the pages of history. Researchers, however, do know what happened to others.

Cinque found that his village had been destroyed and his family had been killed or captured during a war. He briefly returned to the Mende mission, quarreled with the staff, and then vanished. For the next three decades his life was a mystery. Some said he had become a trader or a war chief. Others thought he went to live in the West Indies. No one knew the truth. One day in 1878, a sick old man dragged himself to the door of the Mende mission and claimed to be Cinque. None of the residents recognized him, and the man died before they could ask many questions. He was buried in the mission cemetery, and a black minister—who had once been a slave in the United States—read the funeral service at his grave.

Kale, **Fabanna**, **Kinna**, and **Margru** spent most of their lives at the Mende mission.

Kinna, who had been one of the best English students, often acted as an interpreter. He eventually became a Christian minister and changed his name to Lewis Johnson.

Margru returned to the United States, finished her education at Oberlin College, and then taught at the Mende mission school in Sierra Leone. Her son attended Yale Divinity School and died in the United States.

John Quincy Adams continued to fight for liberty. In 1844, after an eight-year battle, he persuaded

Congress to overturn the gag rules that had prevented members from officially discussing antislavery petitions. Four years later, on February 21, 1848, Adams suffered a stroke as he rose to speak in the House of Representatives. He was moved to the Speaker's room and died there two days later. At the time of his death, a young lawyer named Abraham Lincoln was serving his first and only term in Congress.

Lewis Tappan retired from business in 1849 and devoted his time to the abolitionist movement and other humanitarian causes. He died in 1873, eight years after slavery was abolished by the Thirteenth Amendment to the United States Constitution. One of the Mende mission stations in Sierra Leone was named Mo Tappan in his honor.

Roger Baldwin served as both a U.S. senator and governor of Connecticut. He fought against fugitive slave laws and (unsuccessfully) urged the Connecticut legislature to give African Americans the right to vote. In 1860, as a member of the Electoral College, he helped cast Connecticut's votes for presidential candidate Abraham Lincoln. He died on February 19, 1863, before the close of the Civil War.

Chief Justice Roger Taney remained on the U.S. Supreme Court. In 1857, in the famous Dred Scott case, the Taney Court ruled that Congress could not prohibit slavery in U.S. territories, and stated that the Constitution and the Declaration of Independence did not apply to blacks. National furor over that decision helped bring about the Civil War.

The *Amistad* committee joined forces with several other groups to form the American Missionary Association. In the United States, the association helped support Talladega, Fisk, Howard, and other colleges for African American students. In Africa, the Mende mission, which they founded and later turned over to another religious group, established a large number of schools in Sierra Leone.

Ruiz and **Montes** were sued for kidnapping the Africans by members of the *Amistad* legal team in October 1839. Both Spaniards were arrested and briefly imprisoned in New York. After friends paid their bail, they returned to Cuba. The Spanish government asked the United States to compensate the two former slaveowners for the loss of their property. No settlement was ever reached, and Spain finally dropped the case after the American Civil War.

The *Amistad* case earned a place in history books because it showed that black Americans could use the U.S. legal system to fight for equal justice. It also gave the American people a vivid firsthand look at the horrors of slavery, and public interest in the captives probably helped increase support for the abolitionist cause.

In the years that followed, abolitionists achieved many of their goals. Slavery was abolished in the United States in 1865, in Cuba in 1886, and in Sierra Leone (which by then included both Mende and Vai territory) in 1928.

In the United States, African Americans were finally granted citizenship when the Fourteenth Amendment was added to the Constitution in 1868, but segregation and racism remained a part of American life. The *Amistad* case was not the end of a struggle. It was the beginning.

APPENDIX

THE *AMISTAD* REBELS

O f the fifty-three Africans who boarded the *Amistad* in Havana in 1839, only about two-thirds returned to Africa. Little is known about most of these people, and most of the information below has been adapted from the brief biographical sketches in John Barber's *A History of the* Amistad *Captives,* published in 1840.

THE MEN

Ba, a rice farmer with a wife and child, was kidnapped by two men while traveling on a road. His first master, a Vai, sold him to a Spanish slave trader.

Bagna, an orphan, was born in Kono territory. He lived with his brother, a rice farmer, before being taken to Cuba.

Bartu, a gentleman's son, was probably born in Temne territory. He was captured by a band of six men on his way home from a shopping trip to another village.

Bau, a farmer with a wife and three children, was kidnapped while on his way to the rice fields.

Berri originally lived in a large town surrounded by a stockade. He was seized by soldiers and sold to King Siaka of the Vai, then to a Spaniard.

Burna (the younger), a Mende blacksmith and rice farmer, was condemned to slavery for committing adultery and seized while traveling along a road.

Burna (the elder) was kidnapped while traveling to a nearby town. He knew a little English before coming to the United States and acted as interpreter during the voyage from Cuba.

Cinque was a married man, the father of three children, and the son of a prominent Mende village elder. He worked as a rice farmer before being kidnapped and enslaved for debt.

Fabanna had two wives and one child. He lived in Mende territory and was captured by soldiers who attacked his village.

Faginna was born in Mende country. He was enslaved for committing adultery, sold to a Mende man, and then sold to a Spaniard.

Fakinna, a married man, the father of two children, and the son of a Mende chief or king, was trapped in the bush by a Mende man who belonged to an armed gang.

Fone (or **Foni**), a married man and rice farmer, was born in a large town in Mende territory. He was captured by two men while going to work. He drowned while swimming near the captives' quarters in Farmington, Connecticut, in August 1841.

Fuliwa (Great Fuli) was born in Mende country and captured when soldiers attacked his town.

Fuliwulu (Little Fuli) was Pie's son and came from Temne territory. Both he and his father were captured by an African and sold to a Bullom man who sold them to a Spaniard.

Gnakwoi, a married man with one child, was born in the largest town in Balu territory. He was kidnapped while on his way to the "gold country" to buy clothes and learned Mende only after becoming a slave.

Grabeau (second in command aboard the *Amistad*) was a Mende rice farmer and trader who dealt in camwood and ivory. He was seized while traveling along a road and sold to pay off an uncle's debt. A short (four foot eleven), energetic man, Grabeau spoke four African languages and was often able to help other interpreters translate the captives' words.

Kale (one of the men who wrote to Mr. Adams before the Supreme Court hearing) was kidnapped while going to town to buy rice.

Kimbo, the son of a Mende gentleman, was enslaved by his king after his father's death.

Kinna was born in Mende country. He was seized by

a Bullom man while traveling and sold to a trader named Luiz at Lomboko.

Konnoma was born in Kono territory and did not speak Mende. Because of his filed teeth and tattooed forehead, some Americans initially thought he might be a cannibal.

Kwong was born in Mende country and enslaved for committing adultery.

Moru was an orphan from the Bandi area. His master, a rich man named Margona who had "ten wives and many houses," sold him to a Spaniard.

Ndamma lived with his mother in Mende country before being captured on a roadway by a gang of twenty men.

Ngahoni, a married man with one child, was kidnapped in a rice field by four men.

Pie came from Temne territory. He hunted leopards and elephants before being captured. His son, Fuliwulu (sometimes called Little Fuli), was also one of the captives.

Pungwuni came from a village located between the Mende and Kono areas. He was sold into slavery by his uncle and spent two years doing farm work for an African master before being taken to Cuba.

Sa, an only child, was kidnapped by two men while walking along a road.

Sessi (or **Si-Si**), a blacksmith from Bandi territory with a wife and three children, was captured by soldiers, wounded, and sold twice before he was shipped to Cuba.

Shule (one of Cinque's lieutenants) was the oldest of the *Amistad* rebels. He came from Mende country and was enslaved for committing adultery.

Shuma, a married man with one child, was taken prisoner during a war and sold into slavery.

Tsukama lived in Mende territory before he was kidnapped. He was sold to a person from the Bullom area and then to white traders.

Yaboi, a married man with one child, was enslaved by Mende soldiers who attacked his town. He spent ten years working as a slave in Africa before boarding the *Teçora*.

THE CHILDREN

Kagne, a girl, was sold because her father did not pay a debt.

Kali, a boy, was kidnapped in a village street.

Margru, a girl, was sold by her father in order to pay a debt.

Teme, a girl, was seized by a gang of men who burst into her mother's house one night. She never saw her mother or any of her other relatives again.

Eleven men, whose names are not recorded, died aboard the *Amistad*. The six men listed below died of disease after reaching the United States.

Fa, September 3, 1839

Tua, September 11, 1839

Weluwa, September 14, 1839

Kapeli, October 30, 1839

Yammoni, November 4, 1839

Kaba, December 31, 1839

NOTES

Works here identified by author will be found fully listed in the Bibliography.

CHAPTER 1. MENDE LAND, WEST AFRICA

On a winter day: For information about this incident, see *Emancipator,* January 16, 1840; Jones, p. 15; Barber, Appendix I; Testimony of Singua, *Records,* National Archives; and Abraham, "Sengbe-Pieh: A Neglected Hero?" p. 22, and *The* Amistad *Revolt,* p. 1.

Chapter 2. The Road to the Coast

All the information about African slavery and the slave trade in this chapter, unless otherwise noted, is derived from Reynolds, pp. 33–37; Cable, p. 114; Mannix, pp. 35, 40; Little, p. 37; Oliver, pp. 116–29; Davidson, pp. 98, 101–106; and Watson, pp. 3–33.

Ja Ja: Davidson, p. 257 ff.

"remarkably kind": Pope-Hennessy, p. 88.

The Chewa: Oliver, p. 118.

The Vai: Conneau, p. 244; and Fyfe, *A History of Sierra Leone,* pp. 156, 250.

King Afonso: Davidson, pp. 158–60.

Chapter 3. Across the Atlantic

At Lomboko: Information about the slave station was taken from *Captain Canot, or Twenty Years of an African Slaver* quoted in Fyfe, *Sierra Leone Inheritance,* pp. 159–61, and Mannix, p. 231. All information about the prisoners from Testimony of Singua and Testimony of Grabeau, *Records,* National Archives; Sturge, Appendix E, p. xlvi; and Barber, p. 25 and Appendix I.

The procedure for loading human cargo: All information about slaving in this chapter comes from Conneau, pp. 81 ff and 208; Mannix, pp. 47–48, 113–19; Reynolds, pp. 47 ff; and Everett, p. 55.

Aboard the Teçora: Description of conditions comes from Sturge, Appendix E, pp. xxxvii–xxxviii and p. xlvi.

one-third of the captives died: Jones, p. 15.

The number of whippings suddenly decreased: Information on the prisoners' treatment and reactions in this paragraph comes from Jones, p. 16.

CHAPTER 4. CUBA

crew was tense: Jones, p. 16.

Approximately ten thousand: Davidson, p. 96.

ten to seventeen dollars' worth: Bemis, pp. 385–86.

It was dark: All information on the *Teçora's* arrival in Cuba comes from Sturge, Appendix E, p. xxxvi; *Emancipator,* September 12, 1839; Barber, p. 19; and Jones, p. 16.

Ten or twelve days later: All information on the backwoods camp and the trip to Havana comes from Jones, pp. 16–17; Wyatt-Brown, p. 205; and Sturge, Appendix E, p. xxxvi.

captivity weakened slaves: Turnbull, pp. 62–63.

"gentlemanly": Barber, p. 4.

"made them open their mouths": For documentation of Ruiz's examination of the *Teçora* Africans, see Sturge, Appendix E, pp. xxxvii–xxxviii; Jones, p. 23; and Testimony of Singua, *Records,* National Archives.

"Fine...fine": Testimony of Singua, *Records,* National Archives.

"a man": Sturge, Appendix E, p. xxxviii.

eyes were full of tears: Sturge, Appendix E, p. xxxviii.

CHAPTER 5. "TRYING TO BE FREE"

salt, rum, and gunpowder: Testimony of "Fuleh," New York *Commercial Advertiser,* October 13, 1839.

With gestures: Jones, p. 24.

"would have their throats cut": Sturge, Appendix E, p. xlvii.

"If we do nothing": Sturge, Appendix E, p. xlvii.

"Kill them all": Jones, p. 25.

All information about the mutiny is derived from Jones, pp. 23–26, and Ruiz and Montes's testimony quoted in Cable, pp. 24–26.

CHAPTER 6. AT SEA

With the exception of the sources listed below, the

information in this chapter has been derived from Jones, pp. 26–28; Cable, pp. 8, 15–16; Sturge, Appendix E, p. xlviii; and Barber, pp. 3–4.

Guards...at the helm: Hartford *Times,* September 7, 1839.

Eveline: New York *Times and Commercial Intelligencer,* August 30, 1839.

"long, low, black schooner": Sturge, Appendix E, p. xxxiii.

"lighthouse": New York *Times and Commercial Intelligencer,* August 30, 1839.

CHAPTER 7. LANDFALL

snatched some gold coins: Jones, p. 124.

Some residents: Jones, p. 28.

dressed in blankets: Deposition of H. Green, November 20, 1839. *Records,* National Archives.

Using signs and a few English words: Roger Baldwin to John Quincy Adams, November 4, 1840. Adams papers.

asked if there were slaves in this country: All details of the encounter from the Deposition of H. Green, November 20, 1839. *Records,* National Archives.

thought it might be a smuggling ship: Jones, p. 3. See also Testimony of Dr. Sharp, *Records,* National Archives.

"strange and suspicious-looking": Libel of Lts. Gedney and Meade, December 3, 1840. *Records,* National Archives.

loaded muskets and pistols: Description of the boarding of the *Amistad* from Libel of Lt. Mead [sic]; Deposition of James Ray, December 3, 1839, and Testimony of Lt. Meade, November 19, 1839. *Records,* National Archives.

Montes burst into tears: New York *Times and Commercial Intelligencer,* August 30, 1839.

"Bless the Holy Virgin": Albany *Argus,* September 7, 1839.

"ruthless gang": Sturge, Appendix E, p. xxxv, quoting a thank-you note written by the Spaniards and published in American newspapers.

he silenced the cheering Africans: See Sturge, Appendix E, p. xxxiv, and Barber, p. 5, for a description of Cinque's speeches.

he stared intently; "at intervals he motioned": Albany *Argus,* September 7, 1839.

"uncommon...coolness"; "a composure...of true courage": Barber, p. 4, quoting the New Haven *Gazette.*

CHAPTER 8. ENEMIES AND FRIENDS

"wicked, fearful, bloody bargain": Newmyer, p. 305, quot-

ing a phrase that appeared in the *Liberator* in 1832.

"positive good": John C. Calhoun quoted in Blum, et al., p. 270.

"instituted by God Himself": Sturge, p. 226, quoting the Reverend Mr. Crowther of Virginia.

"hero": Albany *Argus*, September 7, 1839.

"black piratical murderer": New Orleans *Times Picayune*, October 17, 1839, quoted in Jones, p. 84.

"It is the duty of our government": Charleston *Mercury*, quoted in the New York *Daily Express*, September 7, 1839.

prevent other slave revolts: Bemis, p. 388.

"from pirates or robbers": Jones, p. 50, quoting Pinckney's Treaty of 1795.

won the presidency because of Southern votes: Gallagher, p. 2.

stay on good terms: See the discussion of U.S. foreign policy in Jones, pp. 52–53.

New Testament in his pocket: Jones, p. 38.

e-ta, fe-le...: This list of numbers has been taken from Migeod, F. W. H., *The Mende Language*. London: Kegan Paul, Trench, Trubner, 1908. Barber, Appendix I, gives slightly different spellings.

the prisoner was unwilling to talk: Jones, p. 43.

quiet and polite: Cable, p. 28, quoting visitor Joshua Leavitt.

twisted their new shawls into turbans: Jones, p. 42.

burst out laughing: Baldwin, S., "The Captives of the Amistad," p. 338.

clergymen...were executioners: Cable, p. 30.

"cut their throats": Cable, p. 30, quoting an unnamed witness.

children cried. The men looked drawn: Emancipator, September 19, 1839.

CHAPTER 9. THE CIRCUIT COURT HEARING

One man traveled: Cable, p. 37, citing the Hartford *Courant.*

Tourists...asked: New York *Commercial Advertiser,* September 20, 1839.

"If they don't mean to kill us": Emancipator, September 26, 1839.

Terrified, the children clutched: Emancipator, September 26, 1839.

"every one of us would have done": African Captives, p. 11.

"I say there is no power": African Captives, p. 13.

Personally, he detested: Thompson's statements quoted in *African Captives,* p. 44.

"painful": Jones, p. 74, quoting Judge Thompson.

Chapter 10. Plans and Preparations

the coachman tossed Cinque the reins: Cable, p. 47, citing the New Haven *Herald.*

"quick, shrewd...intelligent": American and Foreign Anti-Slavery Reporter, December 1840.

they begged instructors: Barber, pp. 25, 28.

"talking as fast as possible": Barber, p. 18. See also *African Captives* for a description of this incident.

"event that has occurred since the close of the last century": New York *Morning Herald,* October 4, 1839.

"warrior true and brave": Emancipator, September 19, 1839.

"language, appearance...recently brought from Africa": Deposition of Dr. Madden, *Records,* National Archives.

bitter winter weather: Cable, p. 67.

One of the men cried every day: American and Foreign Anti-Slavery Reporter, June 20, 1842.

"delivery" of the "assassins": Sturge, Appendix E, p. xli, quoting a letter from the Spanish ambassador to the State Department.

Van Buren needed Southern votes: Jones, p. 47; and Bemis, p. 393.

Andrew Judson...racist views: Jones, pp. 96–99; and Cable, pp. 11–12.

"special and delicate": Jones, p. 115, quoting a letter written by the secretary of the navy.

CHAPTER 11. THE DISTRICT COURT HEARING

"just from Africa": Testimony of Dwight Janes, *Records,* National Archives.

"language and manners...recently from Africa": Testimony of Josiah W. Gibbs, *Records,* National Archives.

head high and a blanket: Jones, p. 123.

"Give us free!": Abraham, *The* Amistad *Revolt,* p. 15.

Spectators were spellbound: Jones, p. 123; and Cable, p. 70.

"sagacity...keenness": Cable, p. 70.

"genuine"; "no law...prohibited": Statement of Antonio Vega to Mr. Holabird, January 10, 1840, *Records,* National Archives.

"Now," said the defense attorney: All excerpts from Baldwin's speech are from the *Emancipator,* January 30, 1840.

"born free and still...are free": Jones, p. 130, quoting Judson's decision.

"leaped from their seats"; "We thank you": Barber, pp. 29–30.
"lucid, able": Jones, p. 134, quoting the New York
Commercial Advertiser, January 15, 1840.
"scandalous": Jones, p. 140, quoting a letter from the
Spanish ambassador to the U.S. secretary of state.

CHAPTER 12. "GOD WILLING, WE WILL MAKE YOU FREE"

none of the prisoners felt like working: George Day to
Horace Day, February 1, 1840. Day papers.
all thirty-five men: Information on conditions at
Westville from Cable, p. 80, and Adams, *Diary,*
November 17, 1840. Adams papers.
Pendleton sometimes chained: Jones, p. 158, citing a
letter from Cinque to Baldwin, February 9, 1841.
the prisoners kept their feelings to themselves: All informa-
tion in this paragraph is from a letter from Kale to
John Quincy Adams, January 4, 1841. Adams papers.
Five of the nine Supreme Court justices: See Jones, p. 170,
and Bemis, p. 407, for the possible influence of
Southern sentiments on the Court.
Roger Baldwin...wasn't well-known: Bemis, p. 399; and
Jones, p. 152.
His eyesight was failing: Information on Adams's con-

dition from Adams, *Diary*, November 11, 1840. Adams papers.

"life and death": Adams, *Diary*, October 27, 1840. Adams papers.

"by the blessing of God": Bemis, p. 400, quoting a letter from Lewis Tappan to Roger Baldwin, October 28, 1840.

Adams's family was not: Bemis, pp. 348, 350, 375–6, 396, 400; and letter from John Quincy Adams to Charles Francis Adams, April 14, 1841. Adams papers.

"God willing, we will make you free": Cable, p. 80.

CHAPTER 13. "CERTAIN INALIENABLE RIGHTS"

journalists found out: Jones, pp. 137, 244.

Some abolitionists worried...kidnap the Africans: Jones, pp. 166–9.

"to tell [the] court": Letter from Kinna to John Quincy Adams, January 4, 1841. Adams papers.

"Dear Friend Mr. Adams": Letter from Kale to John Quincy Adams, January 4, 1841. Adams papers.

lamps...burned late: Adams, *Diary*, Adams papers. All information in this paragraph is from entries between December 1840 and March 1841, specifically January 2, 1841, January 12, 1841, January 14,

1841, January 16, 1841, January 30, 1841, and February 1, 1841.

"With deep anguish...abominable conspiracy": Adams, *Diary,* December 12, 1840. Adams papers.

"Oh! how shall I do justice": Adams, *Diary,* December 27, 1840. Adams papers.

Adams reviewed his own arguments: All information in this paragraph is derived from Adams, *Diary,* February 22, 1841 and February 2, 1841. Adams papers.

The following morning Adams was almost sick: Adams, *Diary,* February 24, 1841, Adams papers.

his nervousness suddenly melted: Adams, *Diary,* February 24, 1841, Adams papers.

"sympathy with the white": Adams, *Argument...before the Supreme Court...,* p. 6.

"to Cuba, to be sold": Adams, *Argument...before the Supreme Court...,* p. 71.

"That DECLARATION": Adams, *Argument...before the Supreme Court...,* p. 89.

"surpassed the most raised expectations": Log Cabin, March 6, 1841.

"good legal speech": New York *Commercial Advertiser,* March 19, 1841.

Adams reached the court early and waited anxiously: Adams, *Diary,* March 9, 1841. Adams papers.

"With great haste": Letter from John Quincy Adams to

Roger Baldwin, March 9, 1841. Adams papers.

"The big Court": *American and Foreign Anti-Slavery Reporter* (Extra), March 15, 1841.

"[I am] glad"; "[I] thank": *American and Foreign Anti-Slavery Reporter* (Extra), March 15, 1841.

CHAPTER 14. "I AM VERY GLAD THIS DAY"

Now all the Africans wanted was to go home: Letter from Roger Baldwin to John Quincy Adams, March 12, 1841. Adams papers.

"good country": Cable, p. 110.

"If [American] men offer": Sturge, Appendix E, p. xlix.

Children were especially fond of: Strother, p. 79, describes the Africans' relationship with their neighbors.

"cannibals": Anonymous, *Farmington, Connecticut, the Village of Beautiful Homes*, p. 175.

band of bullies: Incident described in Cable, pp. 123–4.

Ten dollars came from a clergyman's widow. A Vermont farmer: Cable, p. 122.

eight dollars and fifty cents: Cochran, Thomas C., and William Miller, *The Age of Enterprise: A Social History of Industrial America*. New York: Harper & Row, 1961.

"Do American men believe..." "Yes": Cable, p. 121.

workers...donated: Sturge, Appendix E, p. l.

In Northampton...in Hartford: Cable, p. 121.

"We said nothing to them": Sturge, Appendix E, p. li.

aurora borealis... "I think we never see Mendi": Strother, p. 80.

Fone began to brood: Anonymous, *Farmington, Connecticut, the Village of Beautiful Homes,* p. 173; and Wyatt-Brown, p. 217.

skip lessons and ignore their teachers: Cable, p. 122.

"My friends": New York *Commercial Advertiser,* November 27, 1841. In November 1996, this Bible was stolen from the library of Adams's house in Quincy, Massachusetts.

kept a close eye on the ship's navigation: All information about the voyage from the *American and Foreign Anti-Slavery Reporter,* June 1842.

"Nya go-hung ni-engo ha": American and Foreign Anti-Slavery Reporter, June 1842.

BIBLIOGRAPHY

BOOKS

Abraham, Arthur. *The Pattern of Warfare and Settlement among the Mende of Sierra Leone in the Second Half of the Nineteenth Century.* Occasional paper. Freetown, Sierra Leone: Institute of African Studies, Fourah Bay College, University of Sierra Leone, 1975.

_____. "Sengbe Pieh: A Neglected Hero?" *Journal of the Historical Society of Sierra Leone,* vol. 2, no. 2, July 1978, pp. 22–30.

_____. *The* Amistad *Revolt: An Historical Legacy of Sierra Leone and the United States*. Freetown, Sierra Leone: U.S. Information Service, 1987.

Adams, John Quincy. *Argument...before the Supreme Court of the United States, Appellants, vs. Cinque, and Others, Africans, Captured in the Schooner* Amistad, *by Lt. Gedney, delivered on the 24th of February and 1st March 1841. With a Review of the Case of the "Antelope," Reported in the 10th and 12th Volumes of Wheaton's Reports*. New York: S. W. Benedict, 1841.

_____. *Diary and Letters*. Adams papers. Microfilm. Boston: The Adams Manuscript Trust, Massachusetts Historical Society, 1954.

Alie, Joe A. D. *A New History of Sierra Leone*. London: Macmillan, 1990.

Anonymous. *Farmington, Connecticut, The Village of Beautiful Houses*. Farmington, Connecticut: 1906. Microfilm. New York Public Library *Amistad* Collection.

Baldwin, Roger Sherman. *Argument...before the*

Supreme Court of the United States, in the Case of the United States, Appellants, vs. Cinque, and Others, Africans of the Amistad. New York: S.W. Benedict, 1841.

_____. Baldwin papers. Microfilm. New Haven: Sterling Memorial Library, Yale University.

Baldwin, Simeon. *Sketch of the Life and Character of Roger Sherman Baldwin, LLD.* Reprinted from *Great American Lawyers,* edited by William Draper Lewis. Philadelphia: John C. Winston, 1909.

_____. "The Captives of the *Amistad.*" *Papers of the New Haven Colony Historical Society,* vol. 4. New Haven: 1888.

Barber, John Warner. *A History of the* Amistad *Captives.* New Haven: E. L. & J. W. Barber, 1840.

Bemis, Samuel Flagg. *John Quincy Adams and the Union.* New York: Knopf, 1956.

Blum, John M., ed. *The National Experience: A History of the United States,* 6th ed. San Diego: Harcourt Brace Jovanovich, 1985.

Cable, Mary. *Black Odyssey: The Case of the Slave Ship Amistad.* New York: Viking, 1971.

Clark, Bennett Champ. *John Quincy Adams: "Old Man Eloquent."* Boston: Little, Brown, 1932.

Conneau, Theophilus. *A Slaver's Log Book or 20 Years' Residence in Africa.* Englewood Cliffs, New Jersey: Prentice-Hall, 1976.

Crooks, J. J. *A History of the Colony of Sierra Leone, Western Africa.* London: Cass, 1972.

Davidson, Basil. *The African Slave Trade,* rev. ed. Boston: Little, Brown, 1980.

Day, George. Day papers. Microfilm. New Haven: Beinecke Rare Book and Manuscript Library, Yale University.

Everett, Suzanne. *History of Slavery.* Greenwich, Connecticut: Brompton Books, 1991.

Foner, Philip S. *A History of Black Americans,* vol. 1. Westport, Connecticut: Greenwood Press, 1975.

Fredrickson, George M. *The Black Image in the White Mind: The Debate on Afro-American Character and Destiny 1817–1914*. New York: Harper & Row, 1971.

Fyfe, Christopher. *A History of Sierra Leone*. London: Oxford University Press, 1962.

_____, ed. *Sierra Leone Inheritance*. London: Oxford University Press, 1964.

Fyle, C. Magbaily. *The History of Sierra Leone: A Concise Introduction*. London: Evans, 1981.

Gallagher, Buell G. "The *Amistad* Incident and the Founding of the American Missionary Association" in *The Talladegan*, vol. 58, May 1940. New York.

Hughes, Langston, Milton Meltzer, and C. Eric Lincoln. *A Pictorial History of Blackamericans*. New York: Crown, 1983.

Jones, Howard. *Mutiny on the* Amistad: *The Saga of a Slave Revolt and Its Impact on American Abolition, Law, and Diplomacy*. New York: Oxford University Press, 1987.

Lewis, Alonzo N. "Recollections of the *Amistad* Case"

in *The Connecticut Magazine,* vol. 11, 1909, pp. 125–9.

Little, Kenneth. *The Mende of Sierra Leone.* London: Routledge & Kegan Paul, 1969.

Mannix, Daniel P., and Malcolm Crowley. *Black Cargoes: A History of the Atlantic Slave Trade 1518–1865.* New York: Viking, 1962.

McCulloch, M. *Peoples of Sierra Leone.* London: International African Institute, 1964.

Migeod, Frederick W. H. *A View of Sierra Leone.* New York: Brentano's, 1927.

Morse, Jarvis Means. *A Neglected Period of Connecticut's History 1818–1850.* New Haven: Yale University Press, 1933.

Murray, David R. *Odious Commerce: Britain, Spain and the Abolition of the Cuban Slave Trade.* Cambridge, England: Cambridge University Press, 1980.

Newmyer, R. Kent. *Supreme Court Justice Joseph Story: Statesman of the Old Republic.* Chapel Hill: University of North Carolina Press, 1985.

Oliver, Roland. *The African Experience: Major Themes in African History from Earliest Times to the Present*. New York: HarperCollins, 1991.

Osterweis, Rollin. *Three Centuries of New Haven, 1638–1938*. New Haven: Yale University Press, 1953.

Peters, Richard. *Reports of Cases Argued and Adjudged in the Supreme Court of the United States. January Term, 1841,* vol. 15. Philadelphia: 1845.

Pope-Hennessy, James. *Sins of the Fathers: A Study of the Atlantic Slave Traders 1441–1807*. London: Weidenfeld & Nicolson, 1967.

Reynolds, Edward. *Stand the Storm: A History of the Atlantic Slave Trade*. London: Alison and Busby, 1989.

Strother, Horatio T. *The Underground Railroad in Connecticut*. Middletown, Connecticut: Wesleyan University Press, 1962.

Sturge, Joseph. *A Visit to the United States in 1841*. Boston: Dexter & King, 1842.

Thompson, Vincent Bakpetu. *The Making of the African Diaspora in the Americas 1441–1900.* Harlow, England: Longman, 1987.

Turnbull, David. *Travels in the West: Cuba with Notices of Porto Rico and the Slave Trade.* London: Longman, Orme, Brown, Green, and Longman, 1840.

Walton, Perry. "The Mysterious Case of the Long Low Black Schooner" in *The New England Quarterly,* vol. 6, June 1933.

Watson, James L., ed. *Asian and African Systems of Slavery.* Berkeley: University of California Press, 1980.

Wyatt-Brown, Bertram. *Lewis Tappan and the Evangelical War Against Slavery.* Cleveland: Case Western Reserve University Press, 1969.

RECORDS

Records of the United States District Court for the District of Connecticut and the United States Circuit Court for the

District of Connecticut (Record Group 21). Microfilm. Waltham, Massachusetts: National Archives, New England Region (abbreviated to *Records,* National Archives, in the Notes).

The African Captives. Trial of the Prisoners of the Amistad *on the Writ of Habeas Corpus, before the Circuit Court of the United States for the District of Connecticut, at Hartford. Judges Thompson and Judson, September term, 1839* (abbreviated to *African Captives* in the Notes).

NEWSPAPERS AND PERIODICALS

Albany *Argus*
American and Foreign Anti-Slavery Reporter
Colored American
Emancipator
Hartford *Times*
Log Cabin
New York *Commercial Advertiser*
New York *Daily Express*
New York *Journal of Commerce*
New York *Morning Herald*
New York *Times and Commercial Intelligencer*
Richmond *Enquirer*

INDEX

Teçora (slave ship), 18–24, 26, 31, 63, 103
Teme, 81, 84, 99
Thompson, Smith, 52–54
Turner, Nat, 42

U
United States
  president of, *see* Van Buren, Martin
  slave trade outlawed by, 19
  treaty between Spain and, 44, 75–76

See also circuit court; Coast Guard; district court; Navy; Supreme Court

V
Van Buren, Martin, 44, 52, 60–61, 65–66, 72–73, 77

W
Webster, Daniel, 69